500

MW00737457

glitter books

MARILYN

THE LAST 24 HOURS

Allan Silverman

ISBN 1-902588-07-X

Published by The Glitter Books of London.

MARILYN

THE LAST 24 HOURS

ALLAN SILVERMAN

PART ONE

In a photographic session with George Barris of *Cosmopolitan* in July 1962, just five weeks before her death, Marilyn Monroe had stated: 'As far as I'm concerned, the happiest time is now. There's a future, and I can't wait to get to it.'

Monroe was 36 at the time, and the shoot had involved her standing on a Mexican beach, the offshore wind mussing her hair, a champagne glass in her hand as a symbol of the Hollywood highlife with which she was associated. Despite her troubled inner world and the fact that she carried too many dark secrets for her years, Monroe at 36 was anything but used-up. She had that summer done a memorable session for *Vogue*, and interviewed by Richard Meryman for *Life*, she had impressed him not only by her enthusiasm, but her ability to skilfully articulate her feelings. Perhaps it was Monroe the secret reader of Jack Kerouac's <u>On The Road</u> and James Joyce's <u>Ulysses</u> who impressed Meryman to the point of his commenting: 'Her inflections came as surprising twists and every emotion was in full bravura, acted out with exuberant gestures... Across her face flashed anger, wistfulness, bravado, tenderness, ruefulness, high humour and deep sadness.' Meryman goes on to tell us, 'I felt a rush of protectiveness for her; a wish – perhaps the sort that was at the root of the public's tenderness for Marilyn – to keep her from anything ugly and hurtful.'

Despite the fact that Monroe had been dropped by 20th Century-Fox, and was seriously reliant on strong barbiturates like Seconal in order to sleep – she had a twelve-year barbiturate habit – Marilyn's last weeks were optimistic ones. Far from being an out of control tragedian on the threshold of her middle-years, Monroe was facing a surprisingly secure future. She had deals to sign, including an eleven-million dollar contract with Italian film-makers for four films in Italy. Monroe who had been dismissed from the set of *Something's Got To Give* on Friday, June 8, ostensibly for flubbing her lines, was not the discarded femme fatale of popular conception. Her pocket-book revealed that she had accepted lunch and dinner dates for the next two months, as well as having planned a three-day theatre trip to New York City.

Marilyn too had a house to complete. In January 1962 she had purchased an L-shaped, immaculately white, Spanish-style house on Fifth Helena Drive, in Brentwood, an exclusively monied and residentially desirable region of Los Angeles. She had given the house a Mexican feel, with tim masks, an Aztec calendar, serape blankets, 50's motel-type lamps, chunky pine tables, Peruvian trinkets, her taste making concessions for the inevitable tri-level glass bar, a display wall and a small hi-fi. Marilyn had put only casual thinking into the interior design, and had spoken to friends of her intention to work on the house and adjoining garden, in the coming months.

Marilyn who at the time was receiving professional help from a psychiatrist, Dr. Ralph Greenson, had as the year progressed showed signs of cracking up. She was frightened to be alone, afraid of going to sleep, and progressively impulsive in her behaviour. Her hairdresser George Masters recalled the delaying tactics she used to keep him at her home. 'She tried to keep me "accidentally on purpose", he recollected, 'by smearing cream in her hair, just so I wouldn't make a plane. When I was getting her ready to go out she would take nine hours. Not that I worked on her all that time – she just wanted me to be there.'

Her sessions with her psychiatrist were exhaustive to her doctor, and would last four to five hours instead of the standard 50 minutes. Ironically it was Dr. Greenson who became the victim of the sessions, reflecting much later, how he had 'become a prisoner of a form of treatment that I thought was correct for her, but almost impossible for me. At times I felt I couldn't go on with this'. It was Greenson who had persuaded Monroe to go for the part assigned to her in *Something's Got To Give*, and throughout the preproduction phase of the film Greenson extended his psychiatric duties to be in endless late-night discussions with the studio hierarchy at Fox. Greenson's professional back-up for his patient was exceptional, given Marilyn's unreliability and her inability to arrive at sessions on time. Forced to fulfil her contractual commitment to 20th Century-Fox by doing the film *Something's Got To Give*, the reluctant screen goddess, massively underpaid by the terms of her old studio agreement, feigned illness to account for her absences. The film's director George Cukor was so disillusioned by Monroe's disrespect for punctiliousness that he raged: 'Let me tell you something, if you placed Marilyn's bed on the set with her in it, and the set was fully lighted, she still wouldn't be on time for the first shot.'

Monroe had a history of depression, a pathology worsened by her dependency on prescription drugs, and her propensity to combine these with bouts of heavy drinking. Like the younger, but equally self-destructive

Elvis Presley, Monroe was clearly overwhelmed by fame and made dysfunctional by its demands. Both stars took refuge in tranquillisers to cushion their essentially private sensibilities from an invasively predatory media. Rumours that Monroe experimented with the as yet unpublicized drug LSD and attempted to throw herself naked off a 5th floor Hollywood balcony are confirmed by a recently discovered letter still in the private property of D. Frank Hurtense's estate, from which I quote relevant extracts. Compelled to confess the terror she had undergone, and unwilling to confide her secret to Dr. Greenson, Monroe had left a scrawled account of her first trip inside an envelope placed in her co-star Dean Martin's dressing-room. I quote from a document which has never before been revealed to Monroe's millions of admirers. 'Deany, things can't get worse. Please help me. Two nights ago I was mad enough to swallow a drug called LSD at a party. Please don't think I'm a junky. Sleepers yes, but that's where it stops. God knows, it's only Greenson's sleepers. I'd be dead without him. But I took this little pill and went overboard. I stripped in front of the whole party... You can imagine... Then I had this crazy thought that maybe I could fly. It was like being drunk, only fifty times scarier. I dunno how I did it, but I ran out to the balcony, and was about to jump when all these people grabbed me. It was cruel Deany, believe me. I wanted to jump. I needed to. Please help me, and tell me I won't end up in the madhouse. If I told Greenson of this incident he might send me away...'

This distraught note written by Monroe on Feb 12, 1962, suggests the reckless extent to which she was prepared to go in the hope of finding relief from the build up of inner crises. The temerity displayed in risking confession of her altered state to a prestigious co-star indicates just how isolated Monroe took herself to be in the final year of her life.

Monroe's reliance on her psychiatrist extended to his advising her on what friends she should keep, what kind of film parts she should take, the sort of man who was good for her to date, and the necessity for her to work on boosting her downgraded sense of self-esteem. Monroe was unduly self-conscious of what she took to be her intellectual shortcomings, and had over the years come to believe in her image as a dumb blonde bimbo, an alluring sex goddess valued only for the availability of her 36-23-33½ figure.

It was this voluptuous figure for which the dress designer Jean Louis had been commissioned to create a gown for Marilyn to make a memorable public appearance at President Kennedy's Birthday Salute at Madison Square Garden on May 19. Of the famous seam-splitting, clingfilm-contoured dress, Jean Louis commented: 'It was nude, very thin material, embroidered with rhinestones, so she would shine in the spotlight. She wore nothing, absolutely nothing, underneath. It cost about $5,000.' Jean Louis recalled how at one of the fittings Marilyn received a call from

Hyannisport, the site of the Kennedy home in Massachusetts, and that she drank heavily after the call was over. Despite the fact that Marilyn had only to sing 'Happy Birthday' to the President, and was likely to be upstaged by performances by star singers like Maria Callas, Ella Fitzgerald and Peggy Lee, she sat in the bathtub and insisted on rehearsing the song hour after hour. The banal lyrics had been supplemented by a verse written for the occasion by Richard Adler, whose politically correct sentiments were aimed at pleasing the Kennedy brothers, both of whom were to attend the celebrations. With Robert Kennedy and his wife seated with John Kennedy in the presidential box, Monroe's performance had to be delayed until last, as she had grown progressively drunker backstage, and sewn, literally into her dress, was unable to walk. Taking to the stage as the finale, her voice was small and hesitant as she struggled awkwardly with the lyrics. Although Marilyn acquitted herself by completing the song, it was obvious to the 15,000 strong Democratic audience that she was drunk. It was the sensational provocation created by her nude dress which had saved her from a potential debacle. The sleaze element implied by Marilyn appearing in public as a woman sexually used by the Kennedy brothers, and advertising herself in this way was not lost to the President and his intimate circle. That Marilyn could go off the wall and in doing so create a shocking political scandal was the undertone to the seductive innocence of the song she had directed at the President. Both Robert and John Kennedy had every reason to feel perturbed by the spectacle of a Marilyn courting self-destruction in the wake of unrequited love. The Kennedy brothers had sniffed danger, and in the ten remaining weeks of her life Monroe was to feel the heat closing in.

Monroe's incendiary nine-week affair with Robert Kennedy, Attorney General and smart FBI manipulator had begun in June 1962. Ironically, Bobby as he was known to Marilyn had spent his political life endeavouring to clean up the extramarital infidelities committed by his two brothers, Teddy and JFK. Initially Marilyn had found in Bobby Kennedy a sympathetic listener, a man prepared to discuss her problems for hours on the telephone, and someone prepared to enter into Marilyn's fantasies and make love down the line. Monroe who had engaged in affairs with celebrities like Frank Sinatra, Yves Montand, and Arthur Miller was overawed by Kennedy's concern with her predicament as a lonely, insecure woman, afraid of the future, and unable to decide on a direction. The much younger Brigitte Bardot and Kim Novak were by the screen popularity they enjoyed pointing up Monroe's disadvantage to their youthful looks. Monroe was by 1962 in danger of becoming another Judy Garland, the burnt-out-star taking refuge in an inner holocaust of wilful self-destruction. For a brief period the solicitous Robert Kennedy appeared to offer the reliable pillar of support she had always found lacking in men. On February 2, 1962, the day after Monroe had first met Robert Kennedy, she confided her thoughts about the Attorney General in a letter written to her former father-in-law, Isadore Miller. 'Last night,' Marilyn wrote, 'I attended a dinner in honour of the Attorney General, Robert Kennedy. He seems rather mature and brilliant for his 36 years, but what I liked best about him, besides his Civil Rights program, is he's got such a wonderful sense of humour.' That both Robert and even more seriously, J.F. Kennedy were to become involved with Monroe as the months progressed was to drive Marilyn into a state of emotional confusion. Marilyn was both infatuated and scared of the two brothers at the same time.

Private wealth endorsed by political power had given the Kennedy brothers the opportunity to cultivate personal despotism. While both brothers were married, JFK to Jackie Onassis, and Robert to Ethel Skakel, neither had any intention of being faithful to their wives, and neither liked opposition to their marriages by their respective mistresses. Something of the tension that existed between Monroe and Robert Kennedy in their brief conflagratory affair was recollected by Monroe's hairdresser, Mickey Song, who was in charge of her hair at the presidential birthday celebrations. Song remembered: 'While I was working on Marilyn, she was extremely nervous and uptight. The dressing room door was open and Bobby Kennedy was pacing back and forth outside, glaring at us. Finally, he came into the dressing room and said to me, "would you step out for a minute?" When I did, he closed the door behind him, and he stayed in there for about fifteen minutes.'

According to Song a violent argument ensued between the couple, and the Attorney General on leaving the dressing room grabbed Song by the arm and asked him if he liked Monroe. Obviously incensed by sexual possessiveness, Kennedy on hearing Song's affirmative answer, angrily proclaimed, 'Well, I think she's a rude fucking bitch,' before angrily returning to his wife.

Mickey Song's vignette is given added colour by his describing how Bobby Kennedy had left Monroe dishevelled and in need of being made up again. Monroe was clearly tired of being used by men, and if in her initial passion to be part of the Kennedy entourage she had hoped to pull Bobby away from his wife, then she was to find herself facing another refusal. There's evidence that both Kennedy brothers were given to throwing violent tantrums in the presence of women, and neither were prepared to compromise in terms of their libertine propensities.

It took Monroe two hours to recover from her seven-minute appearance at the Birthday Salute, before being escorted to a post-gala party thrown by the theatre magnate Arthur Krim. Two hundred of the most powerful men in America, including the Kennedy brothers were in attendance, and Marilyn still in her nude dress and with her hair combed out, danced with Bobby Kennedy on five occasions, while his wife Ethel looked on stonily. Photographs of the two dancing were later destroyed by Secret Service, and Monroe was to join the Kennedy brothers in a private corner of the room. But it was to be J.F. Kennedy who spent the night with Monroe, and not the jealously obsessed Bobby. Using a private elevator that connected to the basement of the Krim apartment building, the couple escorted by security walked through the maze of tunnels that connected it to the Carlyle Hotel and the private elevator to the Kennedy penthouse.

Monroe is reported to have told friends that J.F. Kennedy was a brutal and totally inadequate lover, who performed quickly for the purposes of self-gratification. Monroe told her friend Robert Slatzer that JFK 'was in and out in a few seconds,' and that 'many times, due to his weak back, nothing happened at all.' To Stephen Papich, Monroe complained that Jack Kennedy was 'less than inspired' as a lover, and that Bobby was 'puny.' So why was Marilyn engaged in an affair with the President, we may ask, and why did she spend several hours in JFK's suite that night, leaving Bobby who she was reputed to have loved in a state of vicarious jealousy? It wasn't just that Marilyn was in love with power, she would never have usurped Jackie's place as the President's wife, it was more that she was plotting revenge, and one which will be apparent as this book progresses. If Monroe in her breathtaking nude dress had been out for a sexual conquest that night, then surely she would have avoided a man she knew to be wholly inadequate as a lover. Why was she also putting herself in the position of playing with lethal fire? White House journalist Merriman Smith who attended the post-gala party, and was seen making entries in his notebook was visited at two-thirty in the morning by Secret Service agents who interrogated him over what he knew about the connection between Monroe and the Kennedy brothers. *Time* magazine were similarly raided by agents and all photos showing the Kennedys and Monroe together at Krim's penthouse were removed from their labs and destroyed. Although Monroe wouldn't have been aware of being constantly monitored by security, she would have realised that getting involved with the Kennedys would place her under threat of death.

Allan Silverman

Monroe hadn't been well all year. Relying on amphetamines when she needed to work, and on Demerol to ease her headaches, a pharmaceutical cocktail reminiscent of the ailing Elvis Presley, Monroe inwardly appeared to be in a state of desperate emotional ruin. Her makeup artists like Whitey Snyder found it increasingly harder to cover up the ravages left by Marilyn's nervous exhaustion combined with the facial evidence of nights spent drinking vodka and champagne to excess.

There is also strong reason to think that Monroe had undergone another abortion in July 1962, and as a probable footnote to the emotional drain made on her by terminating a pregnancy, Monroe had alluded to personal loss in an interview with the photo-journalist George

Barris. 'A woman must have to love a man with all her heart to have his child,' she had commented. 'I mean, especially when she's not married to him. And when a man leaves a woman when she tells him she's going to have his baby, when he doesn't marry her, that must hurt a woman very much, deep down inside.'

Marilyn wasn't saying anything new, rather she was speaking for all women by the simple honesty of her sentiments. In 1955 Marilyn had told her friends Amy Greene and Henry Rosenfeld that she had just then undergone her thirteenth abortion, and when on July 19 she checked in for a day and a half at the Cedars of Lebanon Hospital under an assumed name it is more than probable she was terminating the child of either Jack or Bobby

Kennedy. In the process of arriving at hospital Marilyn managed to elude two private detectives who had been paid by Fred Otash to follow her. Marilyn who was a compulsive confider of her private life to an endless series of spiral notebooks, notebooks intended as the blueprint to an autobiography, would doubtless have committed her trauma to paper. Marilyn's notebooks, like so much other potentially damaging evidence were destroyed in the cover-up immediately after her death.

But let's go back in time to May 21, a mere thirty-three hours after the President's gala. Monroe reported for work at 6.15 A.M. on Monday, and gave word to her director, George Cukor that she was up for filming any one of seven upcoming scenes. With her co-star Dean

Martin ill with a throat infection, and Monroe having difficulties in remembering her lines, events were hotted up when Monroe agreed to do the swimming scene nude. Marilyn had told an enthusiastic reporter: 'Thirty-six is just great when kids twelve to sixteen still whistle. You know, I am in better shape than I've ever been in. My body looks better now than when I was a young girl.' And in a highly exhibitionistic night session for *Vogue*, at the Bel-Air Hotel, Marilyn had posed naked in furs and nude behind a screen in what would be the first nude scene by a major Hollywood star. While the stunt was to have appeared spontaneous and unrehearsed, the photographers Larry Schiller and Billy Woodfield were on location to take shots of Monroe which instigated an international bidding war for the racy photos, which in turn was to net the two photographers a sum in the region of one hundred and fifty thousand dollars. Using motor-driven Nikons capable of taking dozens of frames per second, Monroe was shot head-on, from the sides, and slightly above, so as to capture multiple planes of her nude body. Monroe who had begun the scene in an invisible bikini cut form the same bolt of silk soufflé used for her transparent dress at JFK's birthday gala, was at a given point told to deposit the bikini at the side of the pool. The photographers teased the outré sexual extroversion from Marilyn, and while unwilling to be caught out totally nude, she provided the cameras with a zone by zone vocabulary of her sensational body. Makeup artists and hairdressers fought to keep Monroe looking good during her hours spent in chlorinated water. Bunny Gardell coated Marilyn's body in a gel invented by Max Factor for use in water, and a spray was used to keep Monroe's saturated hair looking stiff and brittle. And Monroe knew her worth over the altogether inferior looking Elisabeth Taylor, who had attempted a nude scene in *Cleopatra*, when she told Larry Schiller: 'The week these pictures are released, I don't want to see Elisabeth Taylor's face on any magazine cover in the world.' Schiller gave Monroe absolute right of veto over photographs used, and recalled 'sitting in my T-bird with Marilyn, she with a bottle of Dom Pérignon and a pair of pinking shears. She used the shears to destroy the negatives she didn't like. I ended up shredding hundreds of pictures on the spot because I wanted to keep her absolute confidence.'

But by Monday, May 28, when Dean Martin was pronounced well enough to continue work with Monroe on the film, Marilyn had reverted to her previous anxiety state, and seemed unable to memorise the two words required of her, 'Nick darling,' to the point of making a bad situation worse by running off the set. In her desperation Marilyn believed that only Frank Sinatra could help her, and with a scarlet Chanel lipstick she scrawled several times the words 'Frank, help me,' as a blind appeal to her former lover who was on tour in Australia.

Monroe in a state of inner collapse left the set, but was assiduous in joining Larry Schiller later that evening to approve selected negatives from her nude scene. Marilyn delighted in the planes of her naked body revealed by the photographer, and was in high spirits as she sat in Schiller's car making her selection of frames to be eliminated. That done, Marilyn jumped into her limousine and headed towards Brentwood, but not before telling Schiller that she intended to wear the nude bikini again for a particular lover. Then she disappeared for seventy-two hours without trace. Phone calls went unanswered and dinner-dates were missed. With Dr. Greenson away in Switzerland, where his wife was receiving treatment, and Monroe denied access to her psychiatrist, the crisis she went through on May 26 and 27 would have been magnified by her sense of isolation.

Tabloid rumours at the time had Monroe

tripping on LSD with the psychedelic guru Timothy Leary, undergoing an abortion, checking into an asylum, going mad, and any number of luridly speculative fantasies that seemed to fit with her troubled lifestyle. But the root of Marilyn's troubles that weekend lay in her relations with the Kennedy brothers. We know that Frank Sinatra, who was also to be summarily dropped by the President on account of his underworld connections, had called Monroe advising her against further intimacy with the Kennedys. The suggestion is that Sinatra was asked by the President to break the news to her that her calls would no longer be received by the Oval Office switchboard. FBI director J. Edgar Hoover had met with Kennedy on May 24 ostensibly to advise him that his relations with Monroe could conceivably bring down the presidency if there was to be a leakage to the media. Hoover had also prepared three reports on Sinatra – reports detailing that the singer had 'personal ties to ten leading figures of organized crime.' Monroe had also been warned that she was about to be dropped by the Kennedys by her friend Peter Lawford, whose wife Patricia Kennedy Lawford was no less than the President's sister. What we do know is that on May 25 Monroe had tried calling the President's private line in the Oval Office to find that it had been disconnected. When she tried the White House switchboard, operators refused to put her calls through. Monroe was understandably hysterical. Her dreams of being America's First Lady were brutally shattered

Allan Silverman

when Peter Lawford told her bluntly: 'Look Marilyn, you're just another one of Jack's fucks.'

Locked in her bedroom for the weekend in a haze of champagne-fuelled sedatives, it seems from No 223 of the confidential Oval Office conversation, of the 270 archived, that Monroe managed to contact a guarded Robert Kennedy. Without respect for her feelings an irate Bobby can be heard saying: 'We may screw ass, but we don't take up with it. Get out of our lives. The Kennedys don't marry broads. Leave my brother alone.'

This violent affront to the highly emotional Marilyn put an end for ever to her hopes that her sexual charms could win her a permanent place in the President's life. Denied access to Jack, Marilyn pinned all her remaining hopes on winning Bobby. Rejection brought on all her recurrent fears of going mad and that weekend Marilyn felt her sanity in danger of landsliding into the abyss. Pat Newcomb was there to look after her, and to make sure that she didn't on impulse call the press and reveal her relationship with the Kennedy brothers. Peter Lawford had made it very clear to Marilyn that if she went public it would be her end.

On Monday a shattered Monroe arrived at the studio in her limousine, and returned to the set of *Something's Got To Give*. Her acting was bad and reels of film had to be chivalrously destroyed to help save her face.

June 1 1962 was Monroe's thirty-sixth birthday, and it found her on set under the increasingly critical and disillusioned eye of the film's director George Cukor. In the scene being shot Monroe was to pass off the vapid Wally Cox as the man she had shared a desert island with for seven years. When during a break in filming, Cukor observed Monroe holding a glass of Dom Pérignon, he was unable to contain his anger. Monroe was visibly bringing her personal crises to her working space and Cukor was determined to have her fired. Monroe acted out what were to be her last scenes on film, when positioned at the top of a tall staircase, with six white-hot spotlights directed at her face, she danced down twenty-two steps before leaning over an iron railing to pronounce the words, 'Nick, darling!' to Wally Cox positioned below.

With representatives of Fox conspicuously absent from an impromptu birthday celebration arranged for her at the studios, the occasion seemed both forced and artificial. Monroe had genuine reasons to feel disquieted. She was still plagued by a sinusitis infection, her personal life appeared to be in ruin, and although she looked the very image of glamour in a silk blouse and slacks, with a mink beret pinned to the head, there was a hollowness to her manner which suggested she was indeed anticipating the worst.

The process of firing Monroe was put into motion on June 4. With the actress receiving antibiotic injections laced with megavitamins, and with her hold on reality blurred by the use of barbiturates, Monroe was once again too ill to attend a shoot. With Dr. Greenson attempting to placate the studio on the grounds that the star this time was genuinely ill, Judge Samuel Rosenman, Fox's chairman of the board issued orders to the Fox legal department in New York to prepare a dismissal notice as well as a damage suit against Monroe for one million dollars.

Being fired came as a catastrophic shock to the nervously exhausted Monroe. Dr. Greenson broke the news to her, and found it necessary to inject the distraught actress with a sedative... Cukor was adamant in his statements that Monroe was 'not capable of giving a performance at this point.' In Monroe's defence her devastated psychiatrist and adviser fumed: 'You know, it isn't as if she were gold-digging or out partying. They have acted in bad faith.'

In her confused state of mind Marilyn associated her dismissal by Fox with her rejection by the Kennedy brothers, a part of her thinking which was to prove absolutely right. To the discredited star it seemed as if she was the victim of a hate campaign. According to Fox announcements Monroe was 'not just being temperamental,' she was 'mentally ill, perhaps seriously.' Another source said, 'Marilyn hasn't shown up for days, even though she's been out on the town doing the night spots. Twentieth-Century Fox doesn't want her anymore.'

A few days later Monroe was to discover the sinister knowledge that Judge Samuel Rosenman, who had been responsible for issuing orders to the Fox legal department was the law partner of Clark Clifford, President Kennedy's White House Attorney. Bobby Kennedy's telephone records indicate that he called

Rosenman several times just prior to Marilyn's dismissal. A leaked tape which fell into the hands of this investigative journalist has a steely-voiced Kennedy assert: 'Listen Sam. That bitch is dangerous to Jack, she's dangerous to both of us. I want her out and I want her silenced. Get her where it hurts most. Off the set. You've gotta fix this, so that goddamn bitch disappears right out of our lives. Jackie's got a hint of what's going on. Marilyn could cost us the presidency. She drinks, she talks, she's unreliable [break in the tape] and out of her head on pills. We've got to stop her right now. This whole crazy affair has gone on too long. Get rid of her Sam...'

Bobby Kennedy's orders were obeyed to the word. A smear-campaign was put into motion simultaneous with Monroe's dismissal. A week later on Thursday, June 14, Dr. Greenson escorted Monroe to Dr. Michael Gurdin's Beverly Hills clinic, where after taking off her oversize dark glasses Monroe was to reveal a nose badly discoloured from a beating, as well as a purple bruise on her left cheekbone. Monroe was relieved to discover that no bones were broken, but unwilling to disclose the nature of the incident which had led to facial injuries. It was known that she had seen both her former husband Joe DiMagggio, as well as Bobby Kennedy in the week when the assault had taken place, and either could have been responsible for the beating she had suffered. Monroe came from a family history of mental illness. Her grandmother had been diagnosed schizophrenic, and her mother had suffered psychotic episodes. Monroe's own fear of madness had caused her to spend something in the region of $150,000 over a six-year period, so terrified was she of insanity. Now under threat of a ruined career and of serious recriminations from the Kennedys, Marilyn again found herself on the edge of breakdown. At the same time Marilyn's dependency on Dr. Greenson was made increasingly uncomfortable by her feeling that she had exhausted the material relevant to the sessions. In addition to her inner problems, Monroe had a learning disability as well as suffering from Méniére's disease, an ear imbalance characterised by indistinct hearing. Her vulnerability, at its worst during periods of acute stress was being massively exploited by the

Fox/Kennedy camp.

When Dean Martin quit the set of *Something's Got To Give* on account of Monroe's dismissal, his decision to resign made bigger headlines than Monroe's humiliation, and so Marilyn found herself partly screened from disgrace by Martin's refusal to accept a substitute.

Two weeks after Monroe's dismissal from Fox, Bobby Kennedy flew to Los Angeles ostensibly to attend a dinner party at Peter Lawford's beach house, to which Marilyn was invited. On Sunday June 24, the day subsequent to the dinner party Kennedy dressed casually in slacks and wearing an Oxford-cloth shirt drove his white convertible over to Fifth Helena to see Marilyn. Monroe dressed in a flowing green

Pucci hostess gown and with her hair styled by Guilaroff was glammed up in expectation of continuing her liaison with Bobby. The purpose of Kennedy's 90-minute visit in which the couple walked hand in hand round the swimming pool isn't properly known, although it seems likely that Bobby had come to warn Marilyn away from her repeated attempts to contact the President. Monroe had been obsessively calling the White House switchboard and protesting her name when operators refused to put her through to JFK.

Whatever agreement Marilyn had reached with Bobby resulted in the Attorney General making a call to Samuel Rosenman to have Marilyn reinstated to the set of *Something's Got To Give*, and provided with a re-negotiated contract worth a million-dollar deal to her. It seems that Monroe's part of the bargain was to refrain for ever from contacting JFK. The Kennedys were no strangers to enforcing silence with money, and Monroe's pride was temporarily assuaged by the facility with which Bobby had arranged to have her restored to the film and the offending director removed.

Bobby who had ensured a clandestine union between the Kennedy administration and the lower echelons of the Mafia during the Bay of Pigs affair was a highly adept manipulator at keeping the Kennedy family's indiscretions hidden from the media. Not only had he to cover up traces of extramarital affairs including his own, but he had to keep from public notice rumours of orgies in the White House, drunken

Allan Silverman

cocktail parties aboard the presidential plane Air Force One, and outrageous gambling sprees in Las Vegas. Monroe's problem was that she had convinced herself that she was in love with Bobby. Rejected as no more than a dangerous plaything by Jack, and deluded by fantasies of becoming America's First Lady, Marilyn had succeeded in screening off one blank wall only to run at another.

Moreover Bobby had another reason to make repeated visits to the Fox lot in July 1962 in his blue helicopter borrowed from the military. His best-selling <u>The Enemy Within</u> was in the process of being filmed, and the movie was to profile Bobby's attempt to dispense with organized crime in the labour movement.

At a Fourth of July barbecue held at the

Lawford's Bobby, bare-torsoed in jeans, and Monroe, in a Pucci caftan, walked on the beach together at sunset. Whatever Marilyn's hopes of romance, Bobby's bargaining point was that she stay well away from Jack. Bobby also discussed a variety of issues with Marilyn like global affairs, atomic testing and White House secrets. So dangerous were the topics discussed that their conversation became the subject of a national security matter in the FBI document dated July 13, 1962. One FBI agent claimed that under cover of the sea-wall Monroe performed a lingeringly protracted blowjob on the ecstatic Attorney General. According to Peter Lawford's neighbour, Peter Dye, Marilyn not only had the hots for Bobby, but she 'gazed up at him with wonder in her eyes. She was absolutely

Allan Silverman

starstruck.' But neither of the Kennedys had consideration as lovers. Both according to Monroe lacked staying power, and looked only for quick self-gratification. Monroe was to indiscreetly tell the columnist James Bacon, that 'there were no niceties in sex with the Kennedys. It was in and out. No feeling, no foreplay, no romantic conversation.'

It was Monroe's indiscretions about her personal ties to the Kennedy brothers which pushed her deeper into danger as the summer progressed. She had placed calls to JFK and Bobby through the Fox switchboard and in the presence of friends and acquaintances. She liked to tell people, 'I'm calling Jack, you know, Jack Kennedy. The President.' She even asked the designer William Travila to loan her a white ermine cape from the wardrobe department at Fox, so she could impress the Kennedys.

Monroe was at heart a romantic, and while she felt obliged to offer the Kennedys her body, she entertained constant misgivings about her abilities to satisfy men. To Peter Levathes, she poured out her doubts, in the same way as she did with Dr. Greenson. 'I'm a failure as a woman,' she expressed. 'My men expect so much of me, because of the image they've made of me – and that I've made of myself – as a sex symbol. They expect so much, and I can't live up to it. They expect bells to ring and whistles to whistle, but my anatomy is the same as any other woman's and I can't live up to it.'

After Monroe's death, Dr. Greenson was to tell UCLA's Robert Litman: 'I am afraid that

Marilyn was being badly abused in these relationships', and without naming the Kennedys Greenson referred to his client's 'destructive relationship with two powerful and important men in government.' On his part Litman was to report of his conversations with Monroe's psychiatrist that 'Greenson had very considerable concern that she was being used in these relationships. However, it seemed so gratifying to her to be associated with such powerful and important men that he could not declare himself to be against it. He told her to be sure she was doing it for something she felt was valuable and not just because she felt she *had* to do it.'

As Monroe's complicated relations with the Kennedys deepened, and the Cuban missile crisis became profiled on the political horizon, so

Bobby following in the steps of his brother was to disconnect himself from her life. An informant to the FBI, most probably José Bolânos, had imparted to the Bureau that Monroe had discussed significant questions like 'the morality of atomic testing' with the Attorney General. The result was that when on July 17 Monroe dialled Bobby's private phone line, the one that bypassed the Justice Department switchboard, she got a recording: 'You have reached a non-working number at the United States Justice Department. Please check your directory and dial again.'

Bobby's disconnection was an exact repeat of the way in which Jack had forced Monroe out of his life. To add to her state of panicked confusion, Monroe was told by a

---

Allan Silverman

supervising operator: 'That line was disconnected on the orders of the Attorney General and I'm sorry, but there is no referral.'

For Marilyn, her brutal dismissal by both the Kennedys came as the ultimate rejection. Denied access to Jack, she had secretly hoped to marry Bobby, irrespective of the fact that he was already married and denied rights of divorce by his trenchant Catholicism. It was a situation made critical by the fact that Bobby Kennedy had lapsed in security by sending Monroe hand-written notes. Robert Slatzer was to recall Monroe pulling out of her handbag some papers wrapped with a rubber-band. These were apparently hand-written notes from Bobby Kennedy – some of them on Justice Department stationery. Slatzer also tells us that Monroe showed him the red diary she was keeping in which she had made notes pertaining to a number of conversations with the Kennedys in which red-hot political issues were discussed. Monroe claimed that she had kept this diary because of memory lapses, and because she wanted to face the Kennedys as an equal. When Slatzer asked her what she was going to do if the Kennedys maintained their silence, she said: 'I might just hold a press conference. I've certainly got a lot to say.' Marilyn in effect was in a position to bring down the presidency.

Although Monroe had been recalled to the set of *Something's Got To Give* and was in the active process of finalising her new one-million dollar contract with Fox, there were signs of emotional troubles manifesting themselves

---

Allan Silverman

through anorexia. Monroe had begun to live on champagne and pills and to pursue a 600-calories a day diet. Her main and often only meal of the day comprised a 200-calorie breakfast of poached eggs and grapefruit juice. At other times she would settle for a half dozen oysters washed down with champagne.

The main constituents of Monroe's diet throughout July and August 1962 were three ounces of steak, a Librium, a chloral hydrate, a Nembutal and any number of glasses of Dom Pérignon. She regularly suffered bouts of hypoglycaemia, panic and insomnia. Describing her insomnia to Dr. Greenson, Monroe protested: 'Last night I was awake all night again. Sometimes I wonder what the nighttime is for. It almost doesn't exist for me. It all seems like a long, long horrible day.'

Monroe, who suffered from 'sleep fright', as it is psychologically classified, was far from mad. Her terror was that of developing the symptoms of mental illness, a common anxiety state in people who come from a family history of insanity. Her devoted makeup artist Whitey Snyder, tried to help Marilyn conduct a lifestyle more conducive to regular sleep during that last fateful summer. He recollected how 'she would rush home from the studio and jump into bed at six-thirty or seven P.M., sleep for a couple of hours, and then wake up at midnight for the rest of the night. I could never convince her to stay up until ten or eleven and then go to bed when she was tired like normal people.'

Like Elvis Presley, Monroe educated

Allan Silverman

herself in pharmacology. She read up extensively on the drugs she took, particularly barbiturates, and made her formidable range of pill bottles conspicuous on tables in her living room. When she wanted sympathy she would take a high dose of Nembutal, call a friend, and know that even if she were not rescued, there was no real danger. Monroe had no intention of overdosing, and while she played a game of appealing for sympathy through liberal use of barbiturates, her understanding of how much to take without endangering the body had been won not only from drug manuals, but from the expert knowledge of her doctors.

Marilyn's almost naive assumption that the men in her life would never fail her was badly dented when Dr. Greenson was unable to prevent Fox firing her, despite legitimate claims that his patient had been too ill to attend the studio. In the last weeks of her life Marilyn's confidence in her psychiatrist appeared to have left her, and so the double blow dealt by the Kennedy brothers in ruthlessly evicting her from their lives was made all the more intolerable.

Meanwhile, despite Bobby Kennedy's adroitness at covering his traces, word was leaking out of Marilyn's involvement with the President. An anonymous caller to Ted Kennedy's campaign office in Massachusetts in late July warned that 'a picture of Marilyn Monroe and both brothers still existed.' A similar call was made to the Justice Department offering details of a bugging operation on Monroe's house, with the incentive, 'you will be fascinated by the voices you hear on those tapes.'

It's doubtful that Monroe ever seriously considered the political consequences of her relationship with the Kennedys. She was motivated primarily by infatuation with the power that the Kennedys represented, and secondly by the psychological misapprehension that their wealth and strength would shield her emotional vulnerability. And even when Monroe's romantic ideal was squashed flat by the brothers, it was the anger generated by rejection which occupied her thoughts. Monroe was in the months preceding her death too emotionally overwrought to fully realise that she had placed herself in the position of America's most dangerous woman.

For Marilyn as a lover spurned, the issue at stake was one of desperately unrequited love. Her singular intention was to regain Bobby, and not to bring about Jack's political disgrace.

As it was, in need of a break, and unaware that Bobby would be in Los Angeles the weekend of July 27 to 29, Monroe allowed the conniving Lawford to take her away to the Cal-Neva Lodge in Lake Tahoe, a place owned by Frank Sinatra and Sam Gaincana. Monroe was installed in Bungalow 52, as a special guest, and her former husband Joe DiMaggio was also resident in the neighbourhood that weekend. Monroe who two years earlier had engaged in a wildfire affair with Frank Sinatra, was understandably uneasy about the prospects of a weekend interlude at the lakeside lodge. Part of her was still drawn to Joe DiMaggio, and although the couple didn't meet that weekend, for Monroe spent most of the time locked up in a drugged state, his presence was felt by the confused and often distraught Marilyn.

It was Sinatra who had orchestrated the weekend, ostensibly inviting Marilyn to the lodge to discuss her role in the intended film, *What A Way To Go*, which was to co-star Sinatra. Marilyn had little or no idea of the conspiratorial relations between the Lawfords and the Kennedys, or for that matter between Sinatra and the President. Marilyn who had now begun threatening to call a press conference to inform on the way she had been used and abused by the Kennedy brothers, a move that could have run the Democrats out of office, had become the latter party's biggest threat in their run to be re-elected. Neither of the brothers had calculated on how quickly Monroe developed an emotional attachment to a lover, nor had either possessed the psychological sensitivity to apprehend that Monroe for all her star-attraction was a vulnerable woman desperately frightened of ending up alone. That Monroe should have set her aims first on Jack and then Bobby, both of them married and both disrespectful to the women they used, suggests a complete lack of self-esteem on her part. Despite her renowned beauty, Monroe at 36 felt over the hill. The men in her life had never cultivated the intelligent seriousness that was a part of her, and so resigned to the role of self-destructive dumb blonde, Marilyn made herself easily available to the wrong company. Monroe's insecurity was such that the need to be protected by a strong man led to the exaggerated impulse to find refuge with nothing less than the President or the Attorney General, the two most powerful figures in the United States. So too her attraction to Frank Sinatra, another person whose distinctly underworlded Mafia-thrust endowed him with the machismo to which Monroe was ruinously attracted.

Marilyn whose name never appeared on the Cal-Neva register had gone there in the belief that Bobby Kennedy would be joining their party. Wearing her latter day trademark disguise of dark glasses and a black scarf, Marilyn found herself subjected to Peter Lawford's brutally insistent demands that she remain silent for life over her involvement with the Kennedys. Mae Shoopman the cashier at Cal-Neva has told how Monroe was in such a state of fear that weekend that she would sleep with the telephone at her ear open to the switchboard.

There's every reason to believe that Sam Giancana, joint owner of Cal-Neva with Sinatra, and an associate of the Kennedy brothers was there that weekend to threaten Monroe with Mafia reprisals should she leak news of her involvement with the Kennedys to the press. Monroe claimed she had been held prisoner in her room and beaten, while Sinatra and other members of his entourage engaged in various sex acts with her drugged body. It has been authenticated that Joe DiMaggio was seen at the lodge that weekend because Monroe had called for his assistance, but that he stayed at the nearby Silver Crest Hotel, Sinatra having issued orders that DiMaggio wasn't to enter Cal-Neva Lodge. That Monroe was drugged, unconsciously sexually abused and probably beaten was part of the package used to try and intimidate her into a Kennedy-blank. The photographer Billy Woodfield was there to shoot film of Monroe being enjoyed by the Sinatra circle, pictures intended to ensure Marilyn's silence. 'Just fuck the broad stupid and get it on film' were Woodfield's instructions from one of the Kennedy clan.

The FBI's surveillance of Gianca corroborates the shocking story, and a friend of his called Johnny Rosselli is on tape saying to Gianca, 'You sure get your rocks off fucking the same broad as the brothers, don't you,' a reference to Rosselli viewing the photographs in which Cianca is engaged in sex with Monroe.

Monroe's horrifying experiences at Cal-Neva were the initiation rites to the terrible fear that would pursue her throughout the last week of her life. Confusing emotions with politics, and contesting her vulnerability with the Kennedys' indomitable political dynamic, Monroe was too caught up in her sense of hurt and injustice to be able to gain any clear perspective on the life-threatening situation in which she was placed.

Monroe who was in addition suffering the after-effects of an abortion was physically devastated on her return to Hollywood. En route from Los Angeles International Airport Peter Lawford was to ask his driver to stop, while he jumped out and used a pay phone for over twenty minutes as he believed that his house was bugged. That he had been in conversation with the President is verified by Kennedy's incoming calls on Monday morning, July 30, in which records indicate that the President received a call of twenty minutes duration from Peter Lawford at 8:40 A.M. Lawford was undoubtedly responsible for leaking news to the Attorney General that Monroe was planning to hold a press conference to talk about her relations with the Kennedy brothers.

But there were other reasons why Marilyn was anxious to talk. She had recently taken LSD again, and this time in the company of the counter-culture guru Dr. Timothy Leary. According to Leary he found Monroe 'full of contradictions. Funny and playful, but very shrewd. We talked about drugs and I told Marilyn about a project I was setting up in Mexico that summer. She said she wanted to come on down and join us. But she also wanted to try LSD then and there.'

According to Leary who claimed not to have known that Monroe was under intense psychiatric treatment, Monroe offered him two Mandrax from a copious supply and appeared to be in a fragile mental state. Despite Leary's admonition that the drug was not suitable for someone in her anxiety state Monroe insisted on taking it. Leary tells us that 'they drove together to the wide beach at Venice, and walked by the sea in the dark.' Leary in his account insists that Monroe grew elated on the drug; but given

Marilyn's disturbed condition at the time it seems unlikely that she would have experienced a smooth-ride trip. Leary's predisposition to conceive of LSD as a gateway opening to singularly ecstatic vision probably coloured his perception of Monroe's interaction with the drug.

Monroe however was in a permanently confused state of emotional turmoil, a condition exaggerated by her liberal use of prescription drugs, and it's hard in retrospect not to view her psychiatrist Dr. Greenson as being in conspiracy with Kennedy's aides. Monroe was in a position to be set-up as a suicide by her doctor as a way of disguising a murder plan instigated by the Kennedys. Elvis Presley, Brian Jones and Jimi Hendrix, two at least of who were murdered were all set up in a similar way, their much publicized habits serving to smokescreen the facts surrounding their respective deaths. By overprescribing, and by subscribing to toxic psychiatry Greenson was not only playing on Monroe's dependent nature, but also rendering her vulnerable to exploitation and ultimately murder. It's little wonder that by the time of Monroe's last film, *Something's Got To Give*, the actress found herself unable to remember her lines, and often too drug-hazy to arrive at the studio on time. Caught in a vicious circle Monroe appears to have developed IBS, as a consequence of emotional stress, a factor which again contributed to her unreliability during the shooting of *Something's Got To Give*. Again, rather like the invalided Elvis Presley with his dysfunctional colon, Monroe, if we are to trust

Allan Silverman

the autopsical report was suffering from a congested and discoloured colon. According to Monroe's New York internist, Dr. Richard Cottrell, she had episodes of colitis brought on by pressure, and in 1961 was diagnosed as having an ulcerated colon. It was on the claim made by Dr. Hyman Engleberg that tracks found on Monroe's dead body were the result of injections he had given the star for colitis rather than evidence of the hot shot she had received from the Kennedy party, that suspicions of murder were in part quashed.

What must have been Monroe's second acid trip, coming on top of the ruthless threats issued to her at Cal-Neva, precipitated the crisis in which she spent the last week of her life. Her close friend, Peter Lawford, as though preparing the way for Monroe's liquidation was already spreading noise to friends that Monroe had attempted to kill herself at Cal-Neva on July 28. He neglected to say that Monroe had been forcibly injected there, and while unconscious sexually abused by her hosts. After Monroe's death Lawford was to tell the District Attorney: 'she tried to kill herself the night of July twenty-eighth, and she finally succeeded on August fourth.' Lawford's lies, designed in the interests of covering for the Kennedy brothers pivoted on his conviction that Monroe had overdosed due to her losing *Something's Got To Give*, and that a massive decline in self-esteem had led to her August 4 suicide.

Back home in Brentwood, and signally exhausted from the weekend, Monroe called her masseur Ralph Roberts, who came over to work on her taut neuromuscular tension. Rumours of Marilyn's involvement with Bobby Kennedy had leaked into Hollywood society, and Roberts was to tell his client that news of the affair was all over Hollywood. After Roberts had left Monroe placed an eight-minute call to the Justice Department and presumably spoke to Robert Kennedy. To her mind, Monroe must have assumed that she carried the advantage over the Kennedys, for she was now in a singular position to talk of their infidelities. But what we ask were Marilyn's motives in threatening to expose the Kennedy brothers. We know that she was broke at the time; but if blackmail had been her intention, then the Kennedys would presumably have paid. Or if it was Monroe's hope that by applying emotional pressure to Bobby that she would win him for her own, then her instincts were misguided. Nobody can be coerced into a relationship without feeling a high degree of resentment for the other party, and Bobby Kennedy's trademark happily married image was not one that he was about to give up in the face of the Democrats running to be re-elected.

Monroe must have known too that the scandal, if it was to have broken would have had an adverse effect on her career, and could even have led to her being put out of films altogether. Her fired-up motive to expose the Kennedys was more likely the hurt of a beautiful woman speaking, and one who had been played with and rejected by both brothers in turn, rather than a woman seeking to manipulate the direction of politics. Monroe had no need of becoming a cause célèbre, she was already a glamour icon, and as such, assured of her place in the Hollywood legend.

But she was rightly seething. Marilyn had become used to winning her way through sex appeal, and so rejection of the coarse nature she had suffered at the expense of Jack and Bobby Kennedy was in itself an excruciating experience. Peter Lawford's theory that Marilyn was washed up, and subsequently overdosed in order to save her pride bears no correlation to the facts attendant on her last days. Monroe was in her last week in conversation with director J. Lee Thompson about her next proposed film for Fox, *What A Way To Go*, and there were plans for her to do a musical version of *A Tree Grows*

In Brooklyn, and she was in conversation with the composer Jule Styne about the score. Moreover Marilyn had been given September 16 as a date for work to recommence on *Something's Got To Give*. There was everything to prove, and on Tuesday evening, July 31, Monroe invited her makeup artist Whitey Snyder and her wardrobe assistant Marjorie Plecher over to Brentwood to celebrate the news that the couple were to be married. It was on that same evening that Monroe called her dress designer Jean Louis and ordered a six-thousand dollar evening gown that she intended to wear at the opening of the new Irving Berlin musical, *Mr. President*, set for release on September 6 at the National Theatre in Washington. Monroe knew that the President was to attend the occasion, and it was doubtless her intention to upstage Jackie by her choice of gown for the evening.

Whitey Snyder remembers how enthusiastic and optimistic about the future Marilyn was, in much the same way that friends spoke of the ex-Rolling Stone Brian Jones's passion for new projects in the week preceding his murder. But internally Marilyn carried accumulative psychological scars, and it was to the undertow of psychic damage that she turned in the solitary hours preceding the slow arrival of sleep.

After her friends had departed Marilyn brought out her red notebook, and doubtless made further entries concerning her state of emotional confusion over the Kennedys. Although the latter document together with

Monroe's detailed diaries and notebooks were stolen on the night of her death, a number of pages have come into this author's hands, some partially burned and others fiercely slashed. But a number of paragraphs have survived, and I reproduce here for the first time entries belonging to the night of Tuesday, July 31.

Tuesday, July 31.

Worried about my colon. Don't trust the injections. This affair with Bobby's killing me. I can't stand the pain... How does that sonofabitch stay with his wife; when I could give him so much. He threatens me over the telephone. Tells me that if I speak I'll be in for more trouble than I can imagine. Tells me he'll personally see to it that I never get another contract. Jesus, it's

---

Allan Silverman

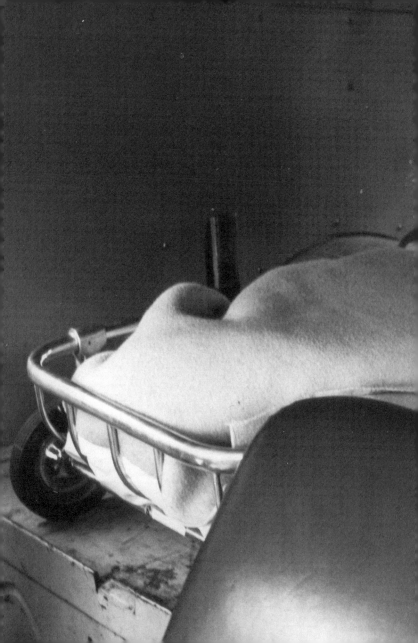

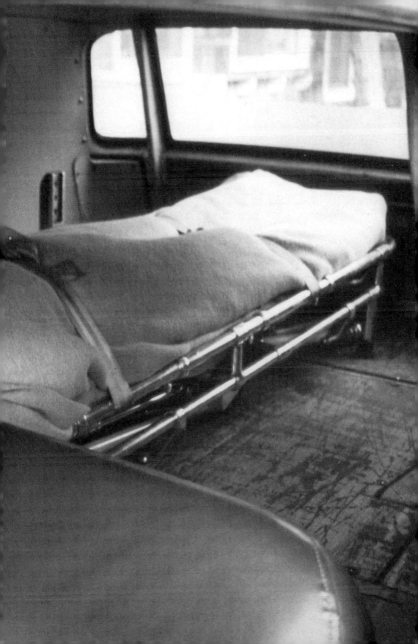

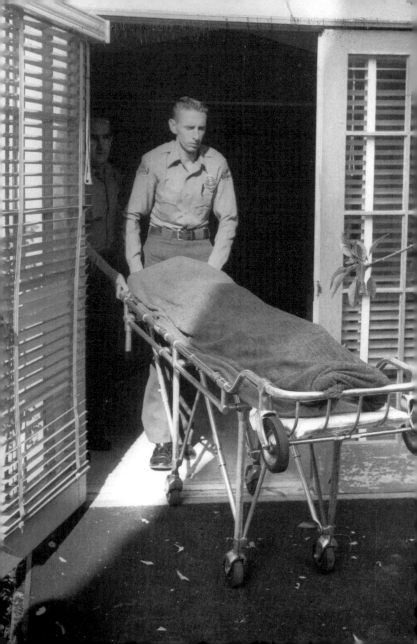

heavy. He means business. I really believe he'd kill me if he could.

Don't need this sort of enemy. He fucks like a wimp, but I love him. Jack too can't keep it up for five minutes. The Kennedys were born bad fuckers...

Called Bobby yesterday. He's furious, but guarded. His voice lets me know I'm in trouble. I've never heard such cold hate. And this is the man who claimed he loved me.

Notes. I've got notes of everything he has told me... Wish he'd shut up bullying me. This'll end bad. I'm not giving an inch. If he comes round here looking for another fuck I won't give in. But I will... I'd do anything to have him for my own. I need a man who can measure up to me and protect me. Sonofabitch.

He's told me too much about Jack and the whole Mafia set up. Hate him. Love him. Hate him. Love him. He got me back with Fox, but at a price. I'm scared tonight. I want to run away and I don't know where to go. Mexico?... Somebody help me. I don't trust anyone.... I'm screaming inside....

Marilyn's state of confusion evidenced by these diary entries supports my theory that her motive was revenge. Her constant oscillation between love and hate of Bobby Kennedy is powerfully expressed in these never before published diary fragments. She hates Bobby for the hold he has on her career, and at the same time she loves him. Despite her vilification of the sexual prowess of both brothers, Marilyn was attracted to the wealth and power which the Kennedys represented. The brothers were after all two of the most influential men in the United States, and Bobby's charisma was infectious in the manner of a pop star's appeal. Marilyn had aimed high, and wasn't now prepared to settle for less.

Monroe who had a history of being used by men – the French actor Yves Montand had conducted an affair with her simply to advance his career – wasn't this time going to be jettisoned because she had become inconvenient. Frank Sinatra had walked through her life, and so too had her former husband Arthur Miller. President Kennedy had recently shut the door on her, and become uncontactable, and now Monroe was unwilling to let go another wealthy playboy.

Monroe too had become increasingly alarmed about the suspicion that her telephone was bugged, and told friends she could hear telltale clicks every time she used her private line. She took to making all her calls to and about the Kennedys from Brentwood phone booths, and in downtown Brentwood bought $400 worth of Chanel No. 5 in respective purchases on the Tuesday and Wednesday of her last week. The perfume was Monroe's favourite, and these comfort purchases pointed to her need to console herself for the emotional stress she was undergoing. Wrapped in a heavy Mexican jumper to offset the cold fog swirling in from the coast, Marilyn also took time to plot out her garden, and to choose dozens of bougainvillaea vines for planting.

Allan Silverman

On the Wednesday evening Monroe invited the Kennedy hair-stylist Mickey Song over to Brentwood, ostensibly to thank him for helping her at the birthday gala. Song who assumed that Marilyn wanted her hair styled, found himself subjected to rigorous questioning about the Kennedy brothers and their wives. Thirty years after the event Song remembered, 'I got the uneasy feeling that she wanted information to use against the Kennedys in some way. She was in a very analytical state – very alert and very determined. She wanted dish, and who else to get it from but the family hairdresser? But I wasn't about to turn on them, not even for Marilyn Monroe.'

Marilyn naturally wanted to know if Jack was happy with Jackie, and Bobby with Ethel, and as importantly whether Song had seen them with 'other women.' Song who didn't know at the time that the conversation was being taped refused to open up, and defended the Kennedys against Monroe's claim that he like everyone else was being used by them. Song's reply to this accusation was, 'They've been wonderful to me.'

Song later claimed, 'she was trying to make it seem as if the two of us were allies against the big, arrogant family. She wanted me to be a co-conspirator.' After Song had beaten a quick exit Marilyn unloaded the reel-to-reel tape on which she had recorded the conversation and hid it in the studio documents in her bedroom. That the tape was stolen on the night of Marilyn's death became clear to Song when he was later confronted by Bobby Kennedy, who said to him: 'You're always defending the Kennedys, aren't you? That's good. I heard a tape Marilyn made of you a couple of weeks ago.' In retrospect Song was to argue Marilyn's side. 'At the time I didn't really care about Marilyn or the Kennedys,' he recalled. 'Now, I think she was abused. They played with her, and they tired of her, and I think they found her a lot of trouble to get off their hands, she wasn't going to go that easily.'

Unknown to Song, and presumably to Bobby Kennedy, Marilyn had earlier that day been guaranteed a million-dollar salary for two films: the completion of *Something's Got To Give*, and for the lead-role in the intended big-budget musical comedy called *What A Way To*

Go. Monroe was to play the part of a rags to riches woman who outlives seven husbands, most of whom dies days after the wedding. She had earlier in the week visited the screening-room at Fox, and sat through two films, *Tiger Bay* and *Flame Over India* made by the British producer-director J. Lee Thompson, who had been proposed to direct *What A Way To Go*. Marilyn had approved of Thompson's work, and so had provided Fox with the go ahead for negotiations.

The stipulations made by Fox were that Monroe should exclude both her drama coach Paula Strasberg and her psychiatrist Ralph Greenson from any further contact with the studio. Fox attributed the failure on Monroe's part to make good in *Something's Got To Give*, to the various and conflicting advice she had received from these two individuals. Her future contract with Fox was contingent on her firing both individuals.

Greenson was glad to be removed from what had proved onerous responsibilities, and Monroe was professional enough to see that her career would advance better without Strasberg's interference. Perhaps as compensation for her own threatened state Monroe lost no time in acting on Fox's contractual demands, and immediately fired the interfering Strasberg, and gave her a one way ticket back to New York. Monroe went further than authorising just these two dismissals from her team, but agreed to replace publicist Patricia Newcomb with Rupert Allan and to discharge Eunice Murray.

Evidently the shock Monroe had received in being temporarily dismissed from *Something's Got To Give* had opened her eyes to the inadequacies of those around her. If Marilyn's personal life appeared to be in ruins, then she wasn't going to let go of her career, and she looked to work as her immediate form of salvation.

Marilyn began the day of Thursday, August 2, by visiting Frank's Nursery in Santa Monica, and as a lover of plants she was to spend all the foggy morning there, both as an admirer and a customer choosing for her Brentwood garden. Dressed in skintight jeans and with her minimal top exposing a bare midriff, she had wrapped herself in a Mexican scrape to resist the early morning cool. Always happy amongst natural things Marilyn was free to discuss the suitability of plants to her garden soil with the Nursery's proprietor.

While in Santa Monica Marilyn visited a bookstore, bought another bottle of Chanel No. 5, windowshopped for shoes and dresses and seemed generally relaxed, before driving over to the Lawford beach house for afternoon drinks. Marilyn arrived with her own bottle of Dom Pérignon and drank it with ice cubes in the glass. Peter Lawford's friend Dick Livingston was at the Lawford's that afternoon and he remembered how on remarking that Marilyn was so pale that she was clearly in need of some sun, Monroe had replied: 'I know. What I need is a tan and a man.'

Still unaware that Peter Lawford was

supplying the Kennedys with the latest up to the minute information about her plans, Monroe as she became mellow from the effects of champagne turned the conversation to Bobby Kennedy's being due in San Francisco the following day. Marilyn's optimistic mood was immediately counterpointed by tension when she spoke of Bobby, and at one point clearly choking back anger Marilyn stormed out of the room and stood alone on the terrace, arms folded and clearly cooling off. Livingston remembered Marilyn being needled to fury by Peter Lawford's failure to disclose whether Robert Kennedy would be visiting with his wife, and whether or not he was due to stay at the Lawford beach house over the weekend.

Marilyn's day was a busy one for she

had invited Whitey Snyder and Marge Plecher over for cocktails and appetizers in the early evening to celebrate the fact that she would be meeting with Jean Negulesco on August 4 to discuss the reincarnated *Something's Got To Give*. Dressed in black slacks and a raw-silk blouse, and redolent of her favourite Chanel Monroe greeted her two guests with glasses of Dom Pérignon. Monroe spoke enthusiastically of returning to the set and of the moral support she had personally received from Darryl F. Zanuck, who had just been named president of Fox. She was excited about the prospects of returning to work, and declared: 'You won't recognize me. Imagine a Marilyn Monroe who actually comes to the set on time.'

But later, after her guests had departed

and Marilyn grew afraid of the coming night, she committed her fears of rejection by Bobby Kennedy to her red notebook. The following extract is from retrieved and partially damaged text.

... He's coming. Bobby and his long suffering Ethel. Already I can smell him, like I do all day after he's visited my bed. Bobby's smell really gets me. It's like damp leaves in a forest.

I don't want him to visit the Lawfords. I want him to drop everything, desert everyone, and come straight to me. What bliss that would be.

... He promised me so much. But so did Jack. When he's angry he wants to fuck me and call me a dumb blonde bitch at the same time.

He hates me for loving him and I love him for hating me. Dumb blonde. My ass! I've read more than him and I know how to mind myself in any company.

I'm afraid of these nights. I know my house is bugged. I've been warned that if I don't destroy everything related to [Jack and Bobby] they'll take action... Every car I hear on the highway at night terrifies me. Can't sleep. Can't read. Can't swallow.

Take pills. Take drinks. Take... My God I'm becoming a nervous wreck. Can't sleep. Call Greenson? No, he's one of them. Think of my Bougainvillaea plants. That'll cheer me.

...If only he'd come and go. I can't stand the strain of knowing he's on the way to California. What if he won't see me. I'll sink into

---

a heap again and need Greenson to pull me out of the mess... Last night I swear someone was watching the house...

If Bobby comes it'll be alright. But it won't. It will. It won't. It will. It won't. He'll shout at me and say I'm a liability to Jack and the Kennedys.

He never listens to me. If I say I'm right he hits me or makes to hit me. Jack's easier, but he's cut off from me by his office. I'm just a broad to Jack. Fucks me in the bath and goes back to Jackie... The lot of women... We're always the ones who are used. Neither Jack nor Bobby have ever asked me about the real Marilyn, the one who lives in the object they desire...

Would I give it all up for Bobby? Yes,

Allan Silverman

I'd become his devoted wife. No, I'd hate myself and him for that. But yes. I'd do it. I'd be his woman today, tomorrow...

I suppose he'd share me with Jack. They think out of one head. I know too much about their dealings. The way they wipe people off planet Kennedy. I've got stuff on tape. It's the tapes he'll come for... He won't mind me. He'll pull the place apart to find evidence against the fucking Kennedys.

... And I've got it, baby. That way he has to see me. He can't avoid asking for the evidence. I'll seduce him. I'll throw him out. He'll fight.

It's late. I'll be a mess in the morning. Don't want to use my pills, but I have to. How did I get like this. Pills for sleep. Pills for

---

working. Pills for my bowels. That's what they call a star I spose... Very tired.... It's already light outside... Sleep...

On Friday, August 3, 1962, Bobby Kennedy accompanied by Ethel and four of the children, jetted into San Francisco. Bobby was in no mood to be humoured, for news of his affair with Monroe had been hinted at by columnist Dorothy Kilgallen in the *New York Journal – American* that day. Kilgallen's column opened:

'Marilyn Monroe's health must be improving. She's been attending select Hollywood parties and has become the talk of the town again. In California, they're circulating a photograph of her that certainly isn't as bare as the famous calendar, but is very interesting...

And she's cooking in the sex-appeal department, too; she's proved vastly alluring to a handsome gentleman who is a bigger name than Joe DiMaggio in his heyday. So don't write off Marilyn as finished.'

Kilgallen's dangerous allusion to Bobby Kennedy as the man in Monroe's life was simply a prefacing detail to the evidence she had been amassing all summer of Marilyn's affairs with the Kennedy brothers. She had interviewed dozens of sources in the Kennedy circle, and Bobby knew that it was only a matter of time before news of the scandal flooded the American nation.

Something of Bobby's visible displeasure at the news was noted by the *San Francisco Chronicle* who reported: 'He was without his

---

Marilyn: The Last 24 Hours   99

usual flashy smile and shook hands woodenly with those that welcomed him. Perhaps the cares of the administration are weighing heavily on him'.

It was a perfect day in California. An offshore wind had made the heat pleasurably tolerable, but Monroe was strung out with anticipation. By mid-morning Marilyn had succeeded in telephoning Peter Lawford's wife, Pat Kennedy Lawford in Hyannisport, and had ascertained from her that Bobby Kennedy and his family had arrived in San Francisco. Monroe had also been told by Pat that her brother's reason for visiting San Francisco was in order to address the American Bar Association in the Bay area, and that the family were due to spend the weekend at the Bates Ranch in Gilroy,

California. In addition to accommodation at a friend's ranch Bobby had secured a top-floor suite at the St. Francis Hotel.

With the obsessiveness of a woman unwilling to countenance rejection Marilyn began repeatedly to call switchboard at the St. Francis Hotel, leaving messages that Marilyn Monroe wanted to speak to the Attorney General. Marilyn was determined to make her affair with Bobby Kennedy public, and excited switchboard operators were quick to relay the news of Monroe's messages to a Kennedy aide. Monroe who was acting out of desperation clearly wanted to force Bobby into meeting at a time when his family were in attendance. And as though to further enforce her image on the shaken Attorney General, glamorous images of Monroe decorated the covers of *Life* magazine and *Paris Match* in their current issues, and *Life* was involved in a special publicity campaign that featured billboard displays of a semi-nude Monroe at newsstands and airport gift shops.

Failing to hear back from Bobby Kennedy Monroe began calling round to her friends threatening to instigate a press conference 'and blow the lid on this whole damn thing.' Asked by her friend Robert Slatzer why she was so intent on going public, Monroe replied, 'I told you I want to her it from him. I want Bobby to end it himself.'

Monroe's insistence that Bobby confront her with news of the end of their affair suggests she hoped that emotions would run high enough to bring them together. It's doubtful that Bobby

Kennedy ever offered Monroe a future, he wasn't in a position to do so, but Monroe was serious and rightly objected to being dismissed from his life without explanation.

Foiled in her initial attempts to reach Bobby Kennedy, Monroe tried to contact the publicist Rupert Allan with a view to arranging a press conference. Allan had just returned from Monaco, and being unwell, wasn't answering calls. Allan remembered: 'I had jet lag after the flight from France and had a bad case of bronchitis I had picked up in Monaco. I knew if I spoke one word to Marilyn, she would insist on coming over with chicken soup and aspirin. And I was really too sick for that.' Speaking thirty years later of events on that hot Friday afternoon in August 1962, Allan was of the opinion that if

Marilyn had called a press conference and exposed the Kennedys it would have been a disaster to her career. Marilyn repeatedly told friends that day that she was in possession of tapes which could ruin the Kennedy image. Bobby of course knew this, but as with any attempt at blackmail he had no idea what existed as evidence against him, or for that matter no assurance that Monroe hadn't copied the tapes and put them in safe keeping. All he knew was that the incriminating tapes were clearly kept at Monroe's house, and that without delay he had to get them into his possession. Monroe's confidence to Peter Lawford that Friday was that 'she had highly incriminating tapes of herself and Bobby,' and that she was prepared to use them if necessary.

Allan Silverman

In the early afternoon Monroe drove to an appointment with her internist, Hyman Engleberg, who reputedly gave her a number of shots to help manage the colitis from which she was suffering. There are no records to confirm what substance Engleberg was using to help combat Monroe's problem, or whether the claim was made simply to cover the needle marks found on Monroe at the time of her death.

Marilyn went on from her internist to her therapy session with Ralph Greenson, stopping on the way to leave several messages for Bobby Kennedy at his hotel. Again unable to reach him, Monroe called Peter Lawford and resumed her threats to ruin the Kennedys. Knowing only too well that Monroe meant business, Lawford in an attempt to placate her suggested that they meet for dinner at an Italian restaurant called La Scala. It has been claimed that Bobby Kennedy made the forty-five-minute flight from San Francisco to Los Angeles that evening, and was seen in the restaurant arguing with Monroe at a back table. That a maître d' at the restaurant distinctly remembers seeing the two at enmity, seated inconspicuously at the rear of the room suggests that Kennedy tried that evening to have Monroe part with the tapes. But if indeed he was planning to kill off their affair, then he would have had nothing to offer in exchange for the incriminating tapes. Seen in this light it's more logical that Kennedy would not have rejected Monroe outright on the Friday evening, for such a move would have been counterproductive to his plan. Marilyn's reported anger may have

Allan Silverman

stemmed from the fact that Bobby once again tried to romance her without any intention of commitment. And Marilyn was probably ignorant still of the violence that could come from Bobby's anger, and of a fanatical devotion to the Kennedy cause that would have nothing stand between him and his objective.

That night as Marilyn struggled with her by now inveterate sleeplessness she received a number of threatening calls from an unidentified woman. Monroe was told to 'leave Bobby alone,' and was repeatedly called a 'slut' and a 'tramp.' Marilyn was sufficiently disturbed by the calls to be up at 6 A.M. and to telephone her friend Jeanne Carmen for emotional support. Carmen suggested that the caller could have been the incensed Ethel Kennedy seeking revenge on

Monroe for the affair she was conducting with her husband. If Monroe taped the calls, which is highly probable, then they were doubtless stolen by the intruders who ransacked her bedroom late on Saturday night.

When Eunice Murray drove to Marilyn's house at approximately 8 A.M. on Saturday morning, it was already eighty degrees. Norman Jeffries arrived at the house half an hour later to begin work on the new kitchen floor and recalled Marilyn coming into the kitchen at about 9 A.M. and looking drained and exhausted. Jeffries remembered: 'she was pale and looked tired. I thought there must have been something wrong with her.' Marilyn was without appetite that day and would only take a glass of grapefruit juice. Marilyn was probably suffering from the stress-

Allan Silverman

related colitis which her New York consultant, Dr. Richard Cottrell had attributed the year before to 'a chronic fear neurosis,' and to recurrence at times when his patient was 'highly nervous, frightened and confused.'

At around 10 A.M. Monroe went outside to attend to the garden, and just generally be with the plants and flowers. Marilyn was weeding when Larry Schiller stopped by to talk to her about photographs for *Playboy* magazine. *Playboy* wanted to use a number of Schiller's nude swimming pool shots of Marilyn in an upcoming edition, and Marilyn who was having second thoughts about the matter asked Schiller to allow her the weekend to make up her mind. Marilyn was understandably hesitant about being promoted as a sex object, and promised to speak to Schiller about the matter on Monday morning.

When Monroe went back into the house she had a run-in with her publicist Pat Newcomb, who had spent the night in Monroe's guest room. The argument seems to have been provoked by the fact that Newcomb had slept well, whereas Monroe had suffered a night of relentless insomnia. But the grievances ran deeper than simply a difference in sleep pattern. Monroe accused Newcomb of loyalty to the Kennedys at her expense. The nature of the altercation that ensued was sufficiently vitriolic for Monroe to fire Newcomb, order her to leave, and then repair to her bedroom and slam the door. According to the housekeeper, Mrs. Murray, Newcomb stayed on at her insistence to have lunch, while Marilyn who refused to eat, kept in her room. Whether Monroe in all probability would have restored Newcomb to her position, once she had calmed down, is a matter of conjecture. Monroe's rages when they did come on were blazingly formidable, and later in the afternoon Bobby Kennedy was to pitch his anger at Monroe's already molten core.

Mrs. Murray was sufficiently alarmed by Monroe's behaviour to call Dr. Greenson, who being otherwise engaged, promised to come over and see his patient later in the afternoon. Monroe's anger had clearly not peaked, for we know of her own admission that Mrs. Murray was fired sometime after making the call to Dr. Greenson. She was told to pack her bags and go by a Monroe who had come to the realisation that Dr. Greenson was now in league with the

Kennedys. Additionally alarmed by Monroe's angry state Murray was to call Greenson a second time, expressing the urgency of the matter, and Greenson promised to come straight over.

Early on Saturday afternoon a giant security helicopter conveying Bobby Kennedy to Los Angeles arrived at the Fox studios heliport and taxied to Stage 14. Studio publicist Frank Neill was surprised to see Bobby Kennedy jump from the helicopter and run to a dark grey limousine parked in the shade and awaiting his arrival. When the limousine door opened and Bobby leapt in, Neill caught a glimpse of Peter Lawford sitting at the wheel. Lawford headed the car through security gates and down Pico Boulevard, then along the Pacific Coast Highway to the Lawford compound. The heat was intolerable, and Lawford's next-door neighbour Ward Wood remembered Kennedy being dressed in Khakis and a white open-neck shirt. For a man who has just been named 'Father of the Year', and who was fast becoming more popular with the nation than his presidential brother, Bobby had everything to loose. As we know it he made calls to Monroe on arriving at the Lawfords in the attempt to placate her, and talk her into parting with the incriminating tapes. Kennedy had undertaken this dangerous journey to Los Angeles scenting the prospects of his own political ruin. He was as desperate as Monroe, but for very different reasons.

What we do know from over forty minutes of the Otash-Spindel tapes covering activity at Monroe's home on that Saturday was that Bobby Kennedy and Peter Lawford arrived at her house in the afternoon, probably an hour before Monroe's psychiatrist called to visit his patient. The tapes suggest that Lawford was a mediator between Marilyn and Bobby, and tried repeatedly to intercede in the violent row that took place between the two hysterical parties. According to Donald H. Wolfe in his book <u>The Assassination Of Marilyn Monroe</u>, 'Marilyn and Bobby had a very violent argument and she told him, "I feel used; I feel passed around". Earl Jaycox, Bernard Spindel's assistant, confirmed that they were shouting at each other. Marilyn was screaming, while Kennedy was yelling, "Where is it? Where is it?" She shouted that she was being treated "like a piece of meat".'

Allan Silverman

The sound-activated tape revealed according to Wolfe's source that 'they were arguing about something that had been promised Robert Kennedy. As they argued, their voices got shriller. If I had not recognized RFK's voice already, I'm not sure that I would have known it was him at this point. He was screeching, high-pitched, like an old lady... He was asking again and again, "Where is it? Where the fuck is it?"' Kennedy was then heard saying, 'we have to know. It's important to the family. We can make any arrangements you want...' Monroe was then heard screaming at the two men, and ordering them out of her house. The episode ended with the sound of a door angrily slammed in her face.

Marilyn was left distraught by Kennedy's

rejection and called her friend Sidney Guilaroff. Speaking in 1984, he remembered her in tears, and her telling him words to the effect of 'Bobby Kennedy was here, and he threatened me, screamed at me, and pushed me around.' According to Guilaroff, Monroe told him of Kennedy's warning 'If you threaten me, Marilyn, there's more than one way to keep you quiet.' Monroe claimed that Kennedy had promised to spend the afternoon with her, but instead had stormed out saying he was going back to Peter's.

Kennedy and Lawford must have left at about 3.45 P.M., for Monroe herself placed an emergency call to Dr. Greenson, who arrived at the house for a ninety-minute session with his patient at approximately 5.00 P.M.

What must have been Monroe's last

Allan Silverman

frantic entry in her journal occurred in the time waiting for her psychiatrist to arrive. The writing is scribbled and manifests real confusion of thought in the sometimes incoherent sentences. I have pieced together some of Marilyn's scrambled attempts to give logic to her chaotic state.

Bobby has murder in his eyes... He would have killed me there and then if Peter L hadn't been standing by. Evil. Evil people. Used me like meat. This time it's all over. Mad. It's happening... I'll go mad like I always feared... But they'll be back. God, I can't take this... Bobby wants to buy me. Wants to fuck me over... with Kennedy dollars. Said he'd do me over... Need to get away... Greenson... About to...

Greenson was to give a number of conflicting accounts of his visit to Marilyn late that afternoon. In a letter to Norman Rosten, Greenson stated: 'I received a call from Marilyn about four-thirty in the afternoon. She seemed somewhat depressed and somewhat drugged. I went over to her place. She was still angry with her girlfriend who had slept fifteen hours that night, and Marilyn was furious because she had had such poor sleep. But after I had spent about two and a half hours with her she seemed to quiet down.' In another account, and much nearer to the truth Greenson stated that Monroe 'had been close to some very important men in government and that she had been expecting one of them that night.'

In still another letter throwing light on

the relationship between doctor and patient, Greenson wrote to Dr. Marianne Kis, two weeks subsequent to Monroe's death that it was Marilyn's intention to terminate her therapy. 'I was aware that she was somewhat annoyed with me,' he wrote. 'She often became annoyed when I did not absolutely and wholeheartedly agree with her... She was angry with me. I told her we would talk more, that she should call me Sunday morning.'

Monroe had claimed to friends that Dr. Greenson was extorting money from her, both in the advisory capacity he had played on her part with Fox, and through the large sums of money he demanded for private consultation. Monroe felt that Greenson had disempowered her to the point of being unable to make any decisions for herself. Greenson was to repudiate her accusations by saying after her death: 'Marilyn was finally making spectacular headway in therapy. She was on her way to achieving a degree of security for the first time in her life. She was really getting better. She knew it, and I knew it.'

In the 723 page report on Monroe's death compiled by homicide detectives it is stated that Kennedy was accompanied to Monroe's house on his first visit by an unidentified doctor, who administered a shot to 'calm her down.' It may have been this first shot, authorised by Bobby Kennedy, and its effects on Monroe which had Greenson claim that Monroe appeared drugged and depressed on his arrival, and remained so throughout their therapy session. And according to Tony Sciacca, a New York investigative journalist, who wrote the book <u>Who Killed Marilyn Monroe?</u> he was granted access to the subsequently destroyed parts of Robert Kennedy's statement, in which the Attorney General admitted to Monroe's having been giving a calming shot in the afternoon. According to Sciacca, 'Bobby told the guys handling the investigation that Marilyn was annoying Jack Kennedy, chasing him and making lots of phone calls to him. He was upset because Jackie Kennedy was bitching and talking about getting a divorce.' Bobby claimed to have brought a doctor to the house with 'an injection to calm Marilyn down.'

Greenson, who was later that night identified as the third man in the Kennedy getaway car driven by Peter Lawford, was ideally placed that afternoon to give Monroe a second shot, or to add chloral hydrate, a colourless, scentless liquid to her champagne. According to Mrs. Murray Marilyn had been drinking champagne all afternoon on an empty stomach, and was sloshed by the time Bobby Kennedy made his afternoon visit. But fear and shock would have sobered Monroe in her vicious argument with Bobby Kennedy, and Greenson who was by this time in contact with Kennedy and Lawford may well have been instructed to continue the sedation of Monroe in the interests of Kennedy and his aides searching the house when they returned later that night.

Greenson's visit to his patient terminated at approximately 7 P.M. According to the psychiatrist he advised Monroe to take some Nembutal and retire to bed, having informed the dismissed Mrs. Murray to stay overnight, and so too Norman Jeffries, who had been working on renovating Monroe's kitchen.

By 9 P.M. Monroe had drawn the black-out curtains, but had left the front windows open. Marilyn spoke to her friend Jeanne Carmen at about this time, and asked her if she would care to come over for a drink. Jeanne declined the offer, as she felt tired, but remembered that 'Marilyn sounded nervous and afraid.'

Some time between 9.30 and 10 P.M. Marilyn's neighbour Elizabeth Pollard saw three men walk down Fifth Helena Drive, and head towards Marilyn's house. According to Elizabeth

Pollard she and her friends 'saw Kennedy go into Marilyn's house just after dusk. They were sitting playing bridge and Bobby Kennedy walked right by the window on his way into Marilyn's house.' Shortly before Kennedy and his two accomplices arrived at Marilyn's door, the actress received a welcome call from her friend José Bolânos, who was calling from a bar in Santa Monica Canyon. Bolânos has never revealed the contents of his conversation with Monroe, only that during the conversation she left the telephone to answer a loud commotion at the door and never returned.

According to Norman Jeffries, he and Mrs. Murray were ordered to leave the house when Robert Kennedy and his accomplices arrived at the house. He remembered, 'we were told to leave. I mean they made it clear we were to be gone... I had no idea what was going on. I mean this was the Attorney General of the United States. I didn't know who the two men were with him. I assumed they were some sort of government men. We waited at the neighbour's house for them to leave.'

From this report, Dr. Greenson seems to be ruled out as the person who gave Marilyn the last fatal injection, for Mrs. Murray would have recognized Marilyn's psychiatrist who had after all visited the house earlier that afternoon. It certainly doesn't eliminate the possibility that Greenson administered a non-fatal hot-shot to Marilyn on his afternoon visit, or that he may have supplied chloral hydrate to Bobby Kennedy to initiate the drug-chain earlier in the day.

At about ten-forty Murray and Jeffries saw Bobby and his two aides leave Marilyn's home. When they returned to the house, they discovered Marilyn in a state of undress lying facedown on the bed, her hand still cradling the telephone. According to Police Sergeant Clemmons, who was not summoned to the house until 4.25 A.M. in answer to Hyman Engleberg's call that Monroe had just committed suicide, 'she was lying face down in what I call the soldier's position. Her face was in a pillow; her hands were by her side and her legs were stretched out perfectly straight... She must have been placed that way. Nobody dies like that.'

Mrs. Murray claims that on returning to the house and assuming that Marilyn was dead, she put through an emergency call to Dr.

Greenson, who said he would be right over, and that Mrs. Murray should immediately call Marilyn's doctor Hyman Engleberg. After alerting Engleberg, Murray then called for an ambulance, but Peter Lawford and Pat Newcomb appear to have arrived at the scene in advance of ambulance drivers James Hall and Murray Liebowitz, who were only minutes away from the Monroe residence when they received the Code Three call.

When the ambulance arrived Hall stated that he placed Monroe on her back on the floor so as to attempt resuscitation. Hall was interrupted in this practice by the newly arrived Dr. Greenson who ordered the removal of the resuscitator and directed Hall to 'apply positive pressure.' According to Hall Greenson then decided to inject adrenaline direct into Marilyn's heart, but the needle hit a rib, at which point Monroe expired. True or false? Hall claimed that he refrained from using the resuscitator on Greenson's demand, because you don't argue with a doctor in a case of emergency. But Hall and his colleague were under no duress to take orders from Dr. Greenson. And would Greenson under scrutiny have deliberately misdirected the adrenaline shot?

According to Sergeant Clemmons Dr. Greenson and Dr. Engleberg had been at Monroe's house for at least three hours before the police were called. What he discovered on his arrival he has called the 'most obvious staged death scene I have ever seen. The pill bottles had been arranged in neat order and the body

---

Allan Silverman

deliberately positioned. It all looked too tidy.'
Clemmons disliked Greenson's attitude, and asked why it had taken three hours to call the police, Greenson replied: 'we had to get the permission from the [Fox] studio publicity department before we could call anyone.'

According to Clemmons a sheet had been pulled up over Marilyn's head, and Dr. Engleberg had seated himself by the bed, with Greenson pointing to an empty container of Nembutal on the nightstand. Clemmons claimed that the body was livid with bruise marks, as though Monroe had been engaged in a violent struggle. But most notable to Clemmons in his initial search of the room was the absence of a drinking glass in the bedroom, without which it would have proved impossible to swallow a bottle of Nembutal tablets. Now in the findings established by autopsy, there was no trace of the distinctive yellow dye in the gelatin capsules in Monroe's digestive tract, something that would have been apparent if she had swallowed seventy or more Nembutal capsules. Monroe had a pronounced aversion to pills and when she did take capsules she usually broke them open and poured the contents into liquid. To have achieved the degree of barbiturates in her bloodstream she would have had to take the equivalent of seventy Nembutal in less than ten minutes, according to a report from the Suicide Prevention Team. The report from UCLA psychiatrist Robert Litman stated that if Monroe had taken the tablets a few at a time she would have been unconscious before achieving the desired aim of an oral overdose.

The most likely form of death in Monroe's instance was death by barbiturate injection. The toxic level in her bloodstream at the time of death was phenomenally high, and Sergeant Jack Clemmons believes that 'Marilyn was given chloral hydrate, a colorless, odorless liquid, in her champagne. It would have worked on her like a Mickey Finn. Then, after she drifted off, the fatal injection of Nembutal was administered.' And clearly injected in the presence of the Attorney General, and most likely under his orders. According to Robert Slatzer, who claimed to have been given access to portions of a secret statement the Attorney General had given William Parker in connection with his movements that night, Bobby claimed that Monroe became 'too distraught to handle.' He also admitted to bringing a doctor who gave the actress 'a mild sedative.' What right this doctor had to administer an injection to someone who wasn't a patient, we will never know.

Marilyn's violent resistance to Bobby on his afternoon visit must have convinced the Attorney General that he would never now persuade Monroe into parting with the tapes. Time was running out for Bobby Kennedy. The first allusions to his affair with Monroe had appeared in print that morning, and it was necessary to stop the leakage at its source.

Other discrepancies surrounding Monroe's death have been pointed up by Peter Harry Brown and Patte B. Barham in their book <u>Marilyn The Last Take</u>. The authors argue against Dr. Greenson's statement that 'nothing was out of the ordinary' on his arrival at Monroe's house, by pointing to breaches in Monroe's inveterate bedtime ritual. Monroe they claim never slept in the nude, but always wore a bra to give her lift. The actress never failed to draw the thick black-out curtains, and would not have fallen asleep with the lights on and the curtains open. Moreover, she always took her sleepers with a glass of milk brought by Mrs. Murray, a habit from which she never departed.

Interviewed later by Sergeant Jack Clemmons, Dr. Greenson was adamant that his patient had no reason to commit suicide. Marilyn's career had taken a radical turn for the better, and she was soon to have received half a million dollars from Fox. But he refused to speak using medical confidentiality as his prerogative. Greenson told Clemmons: 'I cannot explain myself without revealing things I don't want to reveal. You can't draw a line in the sand and say, "I'll tell you this, but I won't tell you that". It's terrible to have to say, "I can't talk about it, because I can't tell you the whole story".'

What appears to evolve from close scrutiny of Monroe's death, is that a number of parties conspired to murder Marilyn in order to ensure the Kennedys' political future. Monroe had been privy via the Kennedy brothers to a U.S. plot to murder Cuban dictator Fidel Castro, according to sources close to the actress, who claimed that Marilyn was killed by the CIA to prevent her from talking. Were the two men

Allan Silverman

observed accompanying Bobby Kennedy into Marilyn's house that night members of the CIA?

Marilyn's last frantic journal entries, retrieved from the general destruction of her papers suggest that she knew her life was in danger. If she had already been given sedating shots in the afternoon at the time of Kennedy's first visit to the house, and again when Dr. Greenson was in session with his patient, then this would explain why Monroe stayed at home, rather than take refuge with friends. Why we ask did the actress sit waiting for her death? Couldn't she have gathered together the items that were so important to the Kennedys, and taken these for the weekend, knowing that her house would be searched in her absence, but that playing for time might have allowed the opposing sides to cool down and renegotiate? If Monroe was already too drugged to take action, then this accounts for her remaining at home, for she was doubtless aware that Bobby Kennedy would come looking again for the tapes and the notebooks, no matter that she had Mrs. Murray and Norman Jeffries on the property. Neither of these two persons represented loyalty or trust in her life. But Monroe waited, in the way that a victim so often becomes magnetized to the victor. We all feel safest in the familiar surroundings which constitute home, and a drugged Monroe had no intentions of leaving.

Dr. Greenson had never before visited Monroe's house for a therapy session, so why did he call that Saturday afternoon? As is standard practice between patient and therapist,

Allan Silverman

Monroe visited her psychiatrist at his residence. What initiated this unprecedented move on Dr. Greenson's part on Saturday afternoon 4 August 1962? In all probability Greenson was in a conspiratorial pact with Bobby Kennedy, and was ideally placed not only to administer an injection, but also to ascertain who was to be at the house with Marilyn on her last night. If Monroe was murdered, as it seems probable, by the cumulative effects of three drug shots, administered by three different people, then each of those three individuals knowingly or unknowingly played a part in her death.

According to Beverly Hills police officer Lynn Franklin, he gave chase to a speeding Mercedes on Olympic Boulevard in Beverly Hills, shortly after midnight. When the car pulled to a stop, and he went over to the driver's side to caution the motorist, he recognized that the driver was actor Peter Lawford. Playing his flashlight into the rear of the car, Franklin was surprised to see that one of the men was the Attorney General, seated next to a third man he later identified as Dr. Greenson. Lawford claimed that he was driving the Attorney General to the Beverly Hilton Hotel on an urgent matter. Franklin waved the car on, and it disappeared into the night.

Monroe's neighbour claimed that they heard the loud reverberation of a helicopter hovering overhead before going off, some twenty minutes after midnight, the indication being that this was the security helicopter flying Bobby Kennedy back from Los Angeles to San

Francisco. Monroe had been injected with enough barbiturate to kill fifteen people, and autopsical findings verified that the barbiturates had bypassed her stomach, and so could not have been orally ingested. The quantity of barbiturate injected made it clear that the intention was murder, unless of course the shot was prepared and administered by an amateur, which is extremely unlikely given the premeditated nature of the crime.

In the time that elapsed between the murder and Dr. Hyman Engleberg's call put through to the West Los Angeles Police Department on Purdue Street, an organized and highly efficient cover up was carried out at Monroe's home. Telephone records were seized, the filing cabinet raided for papers, notebooks and tapes, and a call traceable to Peter Lawford was placed to the White house. All vestiges of the violent scenes which had taken place earlier that night were removed. The bruises on Monroe's body were clearly evidence of her attempts to resist Kennedy and his security officers. Monroe was reported to have carried bruises on her arms, the backs of her legs, with an 'ecchymotic area noted in the left hip and left side of the lower back'.

So died one of the twentieth-century's most loved and enduring glamour icons: a woman who genuinely defined blonde ambition decades before Madonna's PR targeted 'blonde' as an instant selling point. Monroe's romantic impulse, coupled with a desire to link her name to the wealth and power of the Kennedys was to be her undoing. The Kennedy's political machinery allowed for no obstacles, and if Monroe had calculated on the idea of a beautiful woman taking precedence over a Democratic campaign she had misjudged the ideological dynamic. Women were interchangeable to the Kennedy brothers, both of whom regarded Monroe as a desirable, but equally disposable woman. Emotions aren't part of politics, and neither Kennedy brother was in love with Marilyn Monroe. Sadly for Marilyn, they refused to take her seriously, and when she protested over being used, she was coldly murdered.

POSTSCRIPT

Marilyn Monroe's short, sensational and essentially tragic life was one traumatised on her own admission by upwards of thirteen abortions. In fact all the evidence points to her last abortion in the summer of 1962 having been at the instigation of Bobby Kennedy, whose child Marilyn was most probably carrying.

When Monroe lived with Milton and Amy Greene in 1955, she confessed that she had given birth to two babies at a very young age, and that both had been given out for adoption.

One of these children, as we know it through received Monroe apocrypha was a baby girl born in November 1947 when Monroe took refuge at the San Fernando Valley ranch of the actor John Carroll. The girl was placed with the Manisalcos, a family of Sicilian descent living in Brooklyn, and when she grew up she took on the name Nancy Manisalco Greene and insisted she was Marilyn Monroe's daughter. And according to Lena Pepitone, Marilyn's one-time New York maid, the star confessed to her in 1961 that she had given birth to a daughter at the age of twenty-one. Pepitone reported Marilyn as saying, 'I had the baby – my baby! It was wonderful, but the doctor and nurse came in with Grace. They all looked strange and said they'd be taking the baby from me... I begged them, "Don't take

Allan Silverman

my baby!"'

Nancy Manisalco Greene remembered on the tabloid talkshow *Hard Copy* in 1991, that a glamorous woman used to visit her on Long Island in the late 1950s. She knew the woman as Mrs.Greene, and was later told by her grandmother that the woman's identity was the screenstar Marilyn Monroe.

But the more extraordinary aspects of Nancy Greene's revelation are those which carry associations with the controversial Cusack papers. The Cusack papers comprise over three hundred documents, many of them handwritten, pertaining to legal matters between Jack Kennedy and Marilyn Monroe. Although repeatedly declared forgeries by the Kennedy family, these papers discovered in the archives of

Kennedy attorney Laurence Cusack, point towards the likelihood of Jack Kennedy being Nancy Greene's father. Not only are there papers referring to a financial settlement in the form of a trust to be established for Marilyn's mother, Gladys, and her half sister, Berniece, but the compensation according to JFK is in lieu of 'wrongs and broken promises'. Jack Kennedy additionally incriminates himself by expressing concern over Nancy Greene, and Monroe's intentions in 1960 to make the issue public.

Was it a weird conjunction of fates brought Monroe and Jack Kennedy back into a sexual liaison in the last two years of Marilyn's life? Given Monroe's predilection for self-abuse and deeply self-destructive behaviour it wouldn't be incongruous with the psychological patterns

Allan Silverman

of low esteem to conjecture that the attraction to Jack Kennedy was based on the principle of rejection. Initially rejected by the father of her daughter, whose ambitious machinations had seen him rise to the position of President, there's every reason to suspect that Monroe attached herself to the Kennedys in order to face further humiliation. The continued attraction of victim to victor is a common psychological trait in the inherently masochistic. Ruined once, and increasingly fascinated by the testosterone driving the Kennedy brothers, Monroe characteristically recommissioned a need for Jack at the height of his political power. For someone as rejection-sensitive as Monroe her impossible claims on the President provided the ultimate kill-off.

If Jack Kennedy was the father of Monroe's illegitimate daughter, then subsequent research into the sections of the Cusack papers pertaining to Monroe's early life suggests the distinct possibility that Jack's assassin, Lee Harvey Oswald, was the illegitimate son that Monroe gave birth to in 1939 at the age of thirteen.

Monroe who spent the formative years of her life in orphanages, largely due to her mother being diagnosed schizophrenic, left the orphanage for the last time in June 12, 1937, when she was eleven. Marilyn had found a home with the Goddards not far from Hollywood Boulevard, where Grace would take her to the beauty shop, C.C.Browns Ice Cream Parlor, as well as to the movies. Grace Goddard would also

Allan Silverman

take Marilyn to the studios, where her adolescent good looks were much remarked upon. From the Goddards, Marilyn was to move into the care of her Aunt Ana who lived in a duplex in the Sawtede district of West Los Angeles. The move coincided with Marilyn's entry into seventh grade at Emerson Junior High School. According to Marilyn, her 'body was developing and becoming shapely, but no one knew this but me.' But more interestingly Monroe at the time was preoccupied with pubescent sexual fantasies, and recalled in later years, with a degree of literacy that was natural to her, her initial sexual fantasies. 'My impulse to appear naked,' she confessed, 'and my dreams about it had no shame or sense of sin in them. Dreaming of people looking at me made me feel less lonely.

I think I wanted them to see me naked because I was ashamed of the clothes I wore – the never changing faded blue dress of poverty. Naked, I was like the other girls...'

When Marilyn entered the eighth grade in September 1939 she had by then become a busty sex-ideal to the male Emerson pupils. According to Marilyn: 'A few weeks later, I stood in front of the mirror one morning and put lipstick on my lips. I darkened my blonde eyebrows. I had no money for clothes, and I had no clothes except my orphan rig and the sweaters. The lipstick and the mascara were the clothes, however. I saw that they improved my looks as much as if I had put on a real gown... My arrival in school with painted lips and darkened brows, and still encased in the magic sweater, started everybody buzzing.'

Marilyn had in her thirteenth year started accepting dates, and regularly attended school dances, or drive-ins at the Aragon Ballroom on Ocean Park Pier. It was at the latter venue that she first made the acquaintance of Jack Harvey, a sometime lighting technician who had drifted out of studio work into scriptwriting. Jack Harvey remembered Marilyn from the visits she had made to the studio with her aunt Grace Goddard two years earlier. Despite Marilyn's general lack of belief in herself at the time she had clearly made a considerate impression on Jack Harvey.

Harvey who was twenty-two at the time of first meeting Marilyn was a hot-rodder, endlessly souping up the old jalopy he drove around town. Marilyn who was thrilled to be dated by somebody not only connected with movies, but also flash in his lifestyle, at first resisted Harvey's sexual approaches, as she is reported to have done the amatory advances of boys at Emerson Junior High School. Marilyn herself has written of warding off the come-on tactics of a popular ninth-grader, Chuckie Moran. 'We danced until we thought we'd drop,' she remembered, 'and then, when we headed outside for a coca-cola and a walk in the cool breeze, Chuckie let me know he wanted more than just a dance partner. Suddenly his hands were everywhere! But I thought, well he isn't entitled to anything else. Besides, I really wasn't so smart about sex, which was probably a good thing. Poor Chuckie, all he got was tired feet...'

Allan Silverman

But Jack Harvey proved to be more persuasive. Introducing the young Marilyn to the backseat of his car, and subsequently initiating her into heavy petting, he was over the course of two summer weeks in July 1938 to take Marilyn's virginity. Pregnancy was to be the outcome of Marilyn's initial sexual experience and was to be part of the lucklessness that pursued her right down to the last months of her life, twenty-three years later. The lack of precaution taken by the men in Marilyn's life, and their seeming refusal to consider contraception was also a reflection on Monroe's availability to be used. Low self-esteem appears to have been at the roots of her problem.

According to Marilyn's private revelations on three sheets of paper in the

Cusack collection, her first experience of sex was nothing exceptional. 'Jack just wouldn't let up for days...' she wrote. 'He kept on saying what a big thing it would be, how I hadn't lived until I knew what it as life to be (fucked). He was so persistent. Hands everywhere. Got me out of my light summer skirt... and somehow it just started. Jack was gentle. It didn't really hurt. It was kind of strange to have him suddenly moving up and down inside me. I didn't feel anything at first and wondered why he was so breathless and excited. I felt let down. All this girlie talk of what to expect on your marriage night seemed so unreal. I kept waiting for the big event. It was certainly happening for Jack, but not for me.'

The child born in 1939 of Marilyn's fling with Jack Harvey, and subsequently raised by Harvey's relatives in New Orleans, Louisiana, was given the name of Lee Harvey Oswald. We know little of Oswald's early life other than that at the age of 17 he joined the United States Marine Corps, and in 1959, after being discharged from the Marines, he defected to the Union of Soviet Socialist Republics (USSR). An altogether clandestine figure, it is believed that he was informed by an anonymous letter sent to him by Jack Harvey, that his real mother was Marilyn Monroe. It is thought that Oswald received the knowledge shortly before he deflected to the USSR. A document appended to the Cusack papers must have given the Kennedy Brothers some cause for alarm. Marilyn had written: 'I don't think Jack knows that he wasn't the first. There's another, and I'm told he is called Lee Harvey Oswald. Jack Harvey's child. I believe he's got a kink about me. Thinks his famous mother has had a rough deal in life.'

Oswald as we know it returned to the United States in 1962 with his Soviet-born wife and daughter. Oswald must have been assiduously collecting press-cuttings of Monroe's career, and is said to have checked into a Hollywood hotel for two nights in April 1962. Rumour of Monroe's affairs with the Kennedy brothers were by this time common knowledge, and Oswald's realisation that his mother was being deceived and badly treated by the President may well have increased the young man's resolve to assassinate Jack Kennedy. Oswald's obsession with Monroe was verified by the police discovery of a suitcase full of Monroe

Allan Silverman

scrapbooks found in his effects after the Dallas murder. Monroe's death in July 1962, largely believed to have been murder at the instigation of the Kennedys was probably the deciding factor in Oswald's decision to coldbloodedly gun Kennedy down on November 22, 1963, as he rode in the open presidential limousine through Dallas. Lee Harvey Oswald was avenging his mother's death at the hands of the Kennedys.

The story of Monroe's life is one of the most sensational of the twentieth-century. The tragic implications of bearing an early child from the future President of the United States as well as having given birth to his eventual assassin carries with it the very essence of Greek tragedy. That Bobby Kennedy was to be murdered six years later finally brought the wheel full circle.

Monroe's death, still the subject of speculation today was paid for by the Kennedy's with a trail of blood.

glitter books